Original title:
Chasing the Necklace

Copyright © 2025 Creative Arts Management OÜ
All rights reserved.

Author: Ophelia Ravenscroft
ISBN HARDBACK: 978-1-80586-092-1
ISBN PAPERBACK: 978-1-80586-564-3

Tales Woven in Golden Threads

In a box of shimmer and shine,
A squirrel stole my favorite design.
With a twirl it escaped, oh what a sight,
I ran after fluff, in pursuit of delight.

The necklace lay bare, hoping for flair,
While critters conspired, unaware of the snare.
I slipped on a banana, fell flat on my face,
And the gold laughed so hard, saying, 'What a race!'

The Gaze of Time on Forgotten Baubles

Dusted charms on the dresser, they wait,
I swear they conspire, oh isn't that fate?
I blink and they shimmer, 'come show us your style!'
But my closet's the maze where I linger awhile.

Time pokes fun, says 'lost is your flair',
As I dive deep in chaos, with hopes of a pair.
Only to find, as I search for the loot,
That my dog has a taste for a shiny old boot.

Enigmas Adorned in Splendor

A pendant once stolen by trolls, I would swear,
Is hanging 'round necks with an elegant flair.
Every mirror I glance in, it winks with delight,
Yet the trolls keep on giggling, oh what a sight!

A chase through the park, I nearly tripped twice,
For a glimpse of that bling, it was worth the slice.
With giggles and glares from the passersby crew,
I'd say I was bold, but my sneezes gave me clue.

Chasing Reflections in a Crystal Sea

The ocean sparkled with secrets in tow,
Fish flaunted their gems, oh what a show!
I danced on the shore with my hat and my glee,
While seagulls squawked louder, 'They're best left for thee!'

My dreams of a treasure turned hilariously bright,
As waves rolled and tumbled, I took a wild flight.
Splashing around, I forgot all the drama,
With pearls in my pocket and seaweed for karma.

Silken Trails to Radiant Shadows

On a wild quest with a silly grin,
I stumbled over a shoelace pin.
A flash of gold caught my eye so bright,
I danced with glee in the moon's soft light.

The neighbors waved as I tripped and spun,
Searching for treasure, oh what fun!
A cat joined in, with a meow so loud,
We looked like a quirky, clumsy crowd.

Mysteries of the Glimmering Past

Digging through boxes, I found a hat,
Underneath it, a cuddly cat.
A glimmering object, just out of reach,
I lunged forward, a comedic breach.

The cat jumped back with a startled yowl,
As I knocked over a bowl and a towel.
Ancient stories whispered from dust,
As I laughed at my overzealous thrust.

The Quest for a Shattered Locket

In my backyard, my fortress bold,
A secret locket with tales untold.
I waded through bushes, so dense and green,
Where squirrels giggled at my search routine.

I found a sandwich, but missed the prize,
With crumbs on my shirt and a gleam in my eyes.
Maybe this treasure was worth more than gold,
In laughter and crumbs, my fortune unfolds.

Shadows of Antiquity and Glow

As I rummaged through my granddad's chest,
    I wore a top hat, feeling the best.
    An old tin can hid a twinkling thing,
    I posed like a king, ready to sing.

But a raccoon snatched it, oh what a sight,
I chased it down, through day and night.
The laughter echoed, as I danced and leapt,
In search of my glow, while the raccoon crept.

Unveiling the Haunting Fascination

In a shop on the corner, a sparkle caught my eye,
A necklace of wonders, oh my! oh my!
But my wallet was empty, the price was so steep,
I laughed as I plotted, my plans in a heap.

I gathered my friends, we hatched a grand scheme,
To borrow some jewels, oh what a dream!
With capers and giggles, we plotted and planned,
Our antics so funny, we formed a mad band.

We tiptoed through stores, our mission was clear,
But ended up fleeing, filled with belly laughter.
With jewels on our minds, we danced through the night,
As the shopkeepers chased us, it was quite the sight!

In the end, mere pebbles were brought to the light,
Yet still, we found joy in our whimsical plight.
For the chase was the treasure, a memory to cling,
And we laughed till we cried, through our nonsensical fling.

Flickers of a Fabled Elegance

In a dream, I found pearls, they twinkled and shone,
I reached for the magic, but I was alone.
With a grin and a wink, I devised quite a plan,
To dazzle the world while avoiding the man.

I borrowed my grandma's old sewing machine,
Stitched together gems, made a necklace unseen.
With glittering stones from the thrift shop's big sale,
I strutted with pride, but my outfit turned pale.

I wore it with flair, as I strutted my stuff,
Yet, it snagged on my dress – oh, life can be tough!
With each giggle and twist, I embraced the mishaps,
Such elegant chaos, my laughter in laps.

So here's to the glimmer, the fun and the flair,
For in chasing the sparkle, we find the love there.
Life's little treasures are often absurd,
And joy can be found in each silly word.

The Enchantress of Luminous Skies

In the moonlight, a shimmer caught my wandering glance,

An heirloom so tempting, it led me to dance.
I twirled and I spun, it was quite the affair,
But my cat knocked it over – oh, fateful despair!

The necklace rolled wildly, it seemed to have flair,
It bounced on the floor and soared down the stair.
With a laugh and a giggle, siblings did race,
As we barrelled like fools, the chaos embraced.

At the end of the hunt, we found quite a prize,
A habit of trouble that opened our eyes.
For what's worth more, jewels or laughter galore?
The magic was found in the memory's core.

So here's to excitement, the joy of the chase,
With sparkles and laughter, oh, what a sweet race!
In lives lined with jewels, it's the stories we weave,
That shine like the stars when we dare to believe.

Secrets of the Radiant Abyss

A treasure map drawn on a napkin one night,
Said to lead me to wonders, pure jewels, what a sight!
With my trusty old shovel and a handful of cheer,
I ventured in search for hidden jewels dear.

Through gardens of gnomes and slabs of wet mud,
I stumbled and fumbled and fell in a thud!
As laughter erupted from voices nearby,
I found friends united under the sky.

We dug and we dug, but found nothing profound,
Just old rusty buttons and a bottle we found.
Yet the joy of the journey outweighed the lost quest,
With stories we'll keep and giggles expressed.

So let's toast to the folly of vivid dreams spun,
For treasures are plenty when we're all having fun.
In the depths of our hearts, we'll carry the light,
Of laughter and friends as we chase through the night.

The Lure of Gilded Dreams

A twisty road with sparkles bright,
I tripped on dreams, what a sight!
The map was flimsy, made of gold,
The route was silly, truth be told.

With every corner, treasures gleamed,
In my pockets, hopes were beamed.
A laughing cat, a dog in pearls,
I danced through streets, twirled like whirls.

A squirrel stole my woeful hat,
I chased it down, quite full of spats.
With every giggle, laughter soared,
In search of bling, I was adored.

But at the end, just crumbs remained,
In my pursuit, I was entertained.
For gilded dreams can slip away,
Yet joy was found in the folly's play.

Whispers of a Glittering Pursuit

Under twinkling stars we raced,
With laughter strong and dreams embraced.
A map was drawn in crayon bright,
Leading us to the shiniest light.

Through bushes thick and rivers slim,
We sang our hearts out, loud and dim.
A chicken dressed in fine attire,
Joined in our quest, sparked our desire.

We stumbled upon a fountain cool,
Where fish wore crowns, and birds, a jewel.
Each moment filled with silly bliss,
Not one regret, not one lost wish.

Yet when we found the treasure's sheen,
'Twas just a dog with a shiny bean.
We laughed 'til tears rolled down our cheeks,
For in the chase, it's joy we seek.

Threads of Opulence in the Moonlight

Beneath the glow, the threads would shine,
We wove our dreams, oh so divine.
With every stitch, a story spun,
In moonlit night, our hearts had fun.

A goat adorned in shimmering flair,
Led us astray with a cheeky glare.
We hopped and skipped on paths of gold,
In our silly chase, we felt so bold.

A tapestry of giggles grew,
As we chased shadows that danced and flew.
The world of glimmer seemed so close,
Yet laughter reigned, our cheerful dose.

When morning broke, our prize was naught,
Just threads unraveled, mischief caught.
Yet in the chase, we found delight,
In every twinkling, carefree night.

Quest for the Shimmering Adornment

In a land of laughter, we set our sights,
For something shiny to thrill our nights.
With wobbly legs and crazy dreams,
We fumbled on, just giggles and gleams.

A parrot squawked with flair and sass,
As we chased after a shimmering brass.
A frog in shades croaked out a tune,
Underneath the cheeky moon.

We slid through grass and crept through trees,
Our quest was fueled by silly glee.
To find the sparkliest gem in the land,
We teamed up with a ticklish hand.

But when at last, we reached our goal,
It was just a cap from a soda roll.
Yet smiling wide, our hearts were free,
For fun was the treasure, you see!

The Dazzling Mirage

Upon the ground, a shimmer glows,
I trip and slip, oh, how it goes!
A cat dashes past in pure delight,
I laugh at my folly, what a sight!

The jewel sparkles, a playful tease,
It rolls away, just like the breeze.
I chase it down the bumpy lane,
But end up tumbling, what a strain!

Friends gather round, sipping their tea,
"Are you okay?" they quip with glee.
I smile and wink, not feeling blue,
This shiny mischief is worth the view!

With every stumble, the laughter grows,
In this amusing chase, joy flows.
A dazzling mirage, forever bold,
In golden laughter, memories unfold.

Relics of a Stolen Time

A glimpse of gold in the grass I find,
Like clockwork gears, my heart unwinds.
From a pocket, a trinket leaps,
Within the garden, where chaos creeps.

A squirrel steals it, a furry thief,
I run behind, disbelief, belief.
"Hey, come back!" I yell in vain,
While it scampers off with wild disdain!

Time tricks us with its shiny glare,
As treasures hide in thin, cool air.
To catch each glimmer, I need a plan,
But I trip again, oh, yes I can!

Yet in this chase, with every laugh,
I discover gems along my path.
Relics forgotten, a stolen rhyme,
Who knew mischief danced with time?

Jewelry of Forgotten Tales

Old box tucked away, dusty and full,
I peek inside, my heart starts to pull.
A necklace glows, its charm so fine,
But it darts away like a playful vine!

My dog thinks it's a game to play,
Chasing shadows, oh, what a day!
We tumble through tales of a grand old tale,
Together we fumble, together we fail!

A friend joins in, with giggles to share,
As we race through stories, not a care.
With each clipping sound of laughter bright,
The jewelry so precious ignites the night!

Old echoes dance in the laughter's tune,
Another necklace glimmers like the moon.
Forgotten tales scattered all around,
In the wild chase, joy can be found.

Embrace of Radiant Hues

A shimmer whirls like a painted fan,
Across the park, I set my plan.
A vibrant pop, a twinkle, a gleam,
With every step, I just can't scream!

Thumping feet, oh, what a race,
Lost in a game and a merry chase.
The kids all giggle, pointing at me,
As the colors wave like candy from a tree!

A hula hoop flings; I duck and weave,
A necklace catches, yet I just leave.
It sparkles madly, unfolds the night,
An embrace of hues, a playful sight!

Laughter erupts as I stop to rest,
In a sea of colors, I feel so blessed.
Though my treasure remains just out of view,
In this funny chase, I find joy anew!

Glimmering Fables and Lost Trails

In a forest thick with glee,
A squirrel stole my jewelry.
With every turn, I chased it fast,
A glinting tail, a blur, it passed.

Among the trees, I tripped and fell,
My cries rang out, oh what the hell!
The shiny prize, it danced away,
And left me laughing at the play.

Unfriendly bushes snag my hat,
The squirrel stopped, and blinked like that.
It winked and leapt with utmost pride,
As I was left, with nothing wide.

But laughter bubbled in my chest,
As nature's antics played their jest.
A tale of jewels and furry thieves,
Is worth much more than gold, believe!

A Past Adorned in Dazzling Light

I found a ring beneath the stairs,
Not mine, but hey, I've few cares.
A neighbor's laugh rang through the air,
'That's not yours, I swear, beware!'

With shining gems that stole the day,
I donned my grace and strutted sway.
Pretending it was always mine,
A royal mirth, oh how divine!

Yet in the park, I caught a glance,
Of someone else who missed their chance.
I waved and grinned, they spotted me,
Their cheerful scowl, oh what a glee!

A comedy of lost delight,
Where treasures sparkled, gleaming bright.
In fun-filled moments, gold may fade,
But laughter's glow will never trade.

The Essence of Lustrous Gifts

Last Tuesday, while I took a stroll,
A necklace sparkled like a goal.
Determined, I began the quest,
To claim this prize, I must confess.

A cat jumped out and stole the show,
And ran off fast, with jewels aglow.
I laughed and twirled in sheer delight,
As it danced away, a furry flight.

With every turn, the cat would tease,
It wobbled like it owned the bees.
And I would hop, then skip with glee,
'Oh please, just let this shiny be!'

But jewels are dreams, they come and go,
In funny antics, life will flow.
So let the cat keep what it conned,
I'll find a laugh in this fond bond.

An Odyssey of Captivating Glimmers

In a tale where treasures gleam,
I spotted gold; it felt a dream.
A pirate's map, with X on high,
I raced to find it, oh my my!

But every turn led to a laugh,
Where sticks and stones became my path.
A shadow lurked, a glint in sight,
'Twas just a crow, what a silly fright!

I fumbled o'er roots, the swamps did tease,
The treasure chest filled with mud and sleaze.
But through the muck, a spark did shine,
A rubber ring, not yours, but mine!

And so I danced, though not a gem,
With laughter bright, I said, 'Goddamn!'
The quest for riches turns to jest,
For life's rich humor is the best.

Chasing Echoes in Glittering Waters

In a pond so bright, I spy,
Reflections dance and fly,
A shimmering ring slips away,
Oh, how the fish love to play!

With froggy hops and toad-like dives,
I search where the glitter thrives,
Splashing water, without a care,
Laughter bubbles in the air.

A duck quacks loud, what a show,
As I dive in, just for a glow,
The necklace sparkles, fishy and slick,
Swimming around, life's little trick.

Wet and wild, what a great chase,
Frogs giggle in my splashy race,
Oh, what joy in the glimmering light,
Echoes of laughter, what a delight!

In the Wake of Lost Incandescence

In a yard where the daisies bloom,
I spotted a shimmer, dispelling gloom,
A bounce and a waddle, here comes a cat,
Chasing shadows and shiny things, oh, imagine that!

My auntie swings, with her vibrant hue,
Yelling at pigeons, 'It's all for you!'
As I reach for the glint, not a moment too late,
The necklace flies high—it's now a bird's fate!

Twisting and turning, like fish in a net,
I tumble around, but get no sweat,
The sunlight sparkles on paths of grass,
Each laugh a treasure, as I let time pass.

In the end, it's just fun to chase,
A wild adventure in this funny space,
While indigo dreams shimmer so bright,
I'll chase for joy, not for what's right!

Tides of Lustrous Memories

On a beach where my worries flee,
I spy a glimmer far from me,
The tide rolls in like a playful pup,
Sucking my treasure, oh, what a sup!

With footprints squished in squishy sand,
I dance like a crab, not quite planned,
Shells giggle as I search with zest,
For a necklace misplaced, oh, what a quest!

Nearby, seagulls join in the fun,
Flapping their wings under the sun,
With each wave crashing, laughter's roar,
I seem to find joy, who needs more?

At dusk, as the sea whispers low,
Memories twinkle, smiles aglow,
No necklace found, just silly and free,
The tides bring laughter, just like the sea!

The Glow of Forgotten Journeys

In a brimming trunk, so old and wide,
Mysterious treasures start to slide,
I rummage through yarn, dusty and gray,
Finding shiny things lost along the way!

A wink from a gem, a giggle, a spark,
Journeying tales leap out of the dark,
Each trinket a story, a laugh, or a fable,
The glow of forgotten, oh, isn't it stable?

What joy in chaos, finding the past,
I dance with my memories, cheers unsurpassed,
With every wild twirl and each wobbly spin,
Who cares for the necklace? Look what's within!

As laughter bubbles over, it's purely divine,
With sparkly chaos, my heart intertwines,
In every adventure, both silly and sweet,
The glow of forgotten, life's charming treat!

The Pulse of Sparkling Waters

A splash and a dash in the pool so bright,
Hoping to find treasures that twinkle at night.
Caught in a whirl, giggles burst free,
As friends dive in, what joy there will be!

With flippers and masks, they swim like a fish,
Creating a wave, fulfilling each wish.
Amidst all the bubbles, a shimmer they spot,
Was it a necklace, or just a lost pot?

The laughter erupts as they surface anew,
One's wearing a rubber duck—oh, what a view!
Jokes about pearls, the stories they weave,
In this silly quest, no time to grieve.

But wait! What's this? A squeaky surprise,
A toy with a glittery crown and blue eyes.
It's not quite a gem, but still makes them feel,
That sparkly joy is the best kind of real.

Whims of Golden Shadows

In sunlight's embrace, they run through the park,
In search of a trinket, a flicker, a spark.
With shadows that dance, they twist and they twirl,
Each step a new giggle, as ribbons unfurl.

There's Fred in a hat that's far too large,
A crown made of tinfoil—he plays the barge.
With laughter contagious, like ripples on sand,
They'll find what they seek, or craft with their hand.

A glittery object, glinting away,
Could it be treasure? Or just a cliché?
With broomsticks as steeds, they gallop and glide,
In this whimsical quest, there's no need to hide.

But alas, what they find is a dog with a collar,
Fetch and retreat, they all burst into holler!
For on this fine mission, it's clear as can be,
The real joy is found in their silly spree.

Hymn of the Enchanted Splendor

In a forest of giggles, they whisper and roam,
With dreams of baubles, they make it their home.
A squirrel in a tutu joins in on the fun,
With acorns for jewels, oh, what a run!

They search high and low, in bushes and trees,
Losing their hats to the playful breeze.
A sparkling glimpse from the stream down below,
Could this be the prize? They all swirl and glow.

With a leap and a bound, they reach for the light,
To find not a necklace, but a frog in flight.
It croaks a sweet tune, a chorus so grand,
In this magical moment, they all take a stand.

Together they laugh at their wild afternoon,
With certainty sparkling like a bright cartoon.
For treasures are found in the fun and the spree,
In friendship and joy, they're as rich as can be.

The Siren Call of Ornate Echoes

In a land where trinkets gleam,
An echo of a lustrous dream.
Rushing forth with nimble feet,
In pursuit of riches sweet.

With each step, a silly slip,
A wobble, wiggle, double trip.
The glinting prize just out of reach,
With nature's traps they often teach.

Excitement blooms in every chase,
A quirky dance, a comical race.
Around the corner, there it lies,
The treasure shines, a tricky guise.

But oh! A swoop from skies so bright,
A bird snatches it with delight.
With laughter shared, they hit the ground,
For joy in folly, gems unbound.

Beneath the Surface of Shiny Fantasies

In watery depths, they swish and sway,
Gems and jewels at play all day.
Bubbles rise with a wink and nod,
A tangle of dreams, how odd... how odd!

With fins that flash and tails that twirl,
Mermaids giggle as treasures whirl.
Plucking pearls from coral beds,
Jesters in disguise, they smile instead.

Up to the shore, they swim and dance,
A lovely plan, a mishap chance.
Splashing through ripples, laughter peals,
As glittering dreams lose their heels.

But a clam claps shut on a lucky find,
With silly faces, they've been maligned.
Under the sun, they cast their nets,
In the sea of whimsy, no regrets!

Pursuing the Dream of Shimmering Whispers

A glint of light, a whispering call,
Mysteries hidden, they beckon all.
Through winding paths and twisting trees,
The playful breeze teases and frees.

Frogs leap bright, a comedic show,
Chasing reflections, a merry fro.
Giggles erupt with each little hop,
In pursuit of a spark that will never stop.

But what's this? A squirrel in flight,
Stealing jewels under the moonlight.
With haste they run, a chuckle escapes,
A game of jest with glittering shapes.

At journey's end, they find their glee,
For riches lost were meant to be.
With bags of laughter, and tales to spin,
In shimmering whispers, the fun begins.

The Alluring Path of a Stolen Tiara

Beneath the queen's grand gilded throne,
A tiara glints, its sparkle known.
Tiny feet make a sneaky dash,
With hopeful hearts, they make a splash.

Round and round, on merry-goes,
Frolicking where the mischief flows.
The crown takes flight, it's off its head,
A raucous chase, their shoulders red.

Through bakeries with pies in air,
In sticky traps, they dance and dare.
With frosting flung, they share a grin,
A laughter-laden wild, cheeky win.

But in the end, the crown's a tease,
Just a joke spurred on by the breeze.
In jest and fun, they laugh aloud,
For stolen dreams are joys endowed.

Secrets Wrapped in Gold

In a dusty chest, treasures lay,
Some shiny beads and a bright bouquet.
Glimmers dance, what a silly sight,
Who knew old coins could bring such delight?

With every twist, the tale unfolds,
Laughs and giggles over secret molds.
What was once lost, now found anew,
A bracelet here, and a brooch or two!

Old Auntie's giggle, a curious tease,
"Those gems aren't real, they're just for sneeze!"
A jeweled saga, absurd but fine,
Crafted with wit, and some clever line!

Who needs a map when laughter's the key?
To find a gem or perhaps just glee.
With friends around, we chuckle and play,
Unearthing joy in a comedic way!

The Siren's Call of Sparkling Beauty

Beneath the waves, a shimmer bright,
A fish wore pearls, what a funny sight!
With bubbles and giggles from ocean's floor,
It's just a scoop; who could ask for more?

A treasure hunt with a silly twist,
Each find a laugh, none to be missed.
The golden crown of a giggly clown,
A pirate's bling with an upside-down frown!

"Hey! Don't touch that!" said the mermaid bold,
Her necklace glinted with stories untold.
But we swam away for a jellyfish race,
Leaving shiny jewels by the coral base!

At the end of the day, what do we keep?
Silly memories, not treasures that sweep.
With every wave, laughter we spurred,
Life's riches are fun, rather absurd!

Tracing the Stolen Light

In a shop, a sparkle caught my eye,
A rogue in shadows—oh my, oh my!
With all the twinkle, I just had to peek,
But the jewel thief wore quite the cheek!

A game of tag on a glittery spree,
With hoops and loops, come and find me!
Rushed by the door, what a sight to behold,
The necklace jingled, as I got bold!

Around the corner, with a dash and a dive,
What was my goal? Just to feel alive!
But with every turn, I found only clowns,
In sparkly hats and colorful gowns!

Who needs a gem when joy's on display?
I laughed so hard, my woes ran away.
So let them steal the shiny delight,
For fun outshines any jewel in sight!

Odyssey of Lustrous Wonders

Through fields of daisies, we tumbled and ran,
Chasing the glimmers held in a can.
In the light of the sun, we spotted some bling,
A toast to the sparkles! Let the laughter ring!

"Oh look, a gem!" one would decree,
It was merely a button from Grandma's decree.
But our hearts were light as we danced in the sun,
With treasures imagined, adventures begun!

We built a castle from candy and dreams,
With licorice towers, or so it seems.
With a sprinkle of glitter, we crowned the day,
The real riches? The laughter we play!

So here's to the stories and memories made,
With each shiny bauble, our fears would evade.
An odyssey shared, full of wonder and cheer,
No need for gold when friendship is near!

Quest for the Lost Adornment

In a world of fluff and shine,
I lost a sparkly thing divine.
I searched beneath the couch so wide,
What a prize my treasure bide!

A cat named Mittens stole the show,
With jewels upon her furry toe.
Each step she prances, oh so grand,
A dazzling sight, a furry band!

I asked the dog, my loyal mate,
"Did you see it? Oh, it's late!"
He just wagged, not a clue in sight,
But to find that gem, I'll put up a fight!

In bushes, under size-six shoes,
I search in places one would lose.
But laughter fills my frantic quest,
For in the end, it's all a jest!

Threads of Enchantment

With shimmery threads all around,
I stumbled on treasures I'd found.
A string of pearls, a brooch so bright,
But where's that spark? It's quite a fright!

My neighbor's dog has scampered off,
With glittering items, he's the scoff.
I chase him down the winding street,
He barks and twirls, oh what a feat!

But every locket leads to charms,
I swear they all have secret harms.
A frog croaks back, it's all a game,
With stolen spoons and a silly name!

Through tangled vines and silly dreams,
I laugh aloud at how it seems.
In this wild chase for shiny things,
I find the joy mischief brings.

The Hunt for Elegance

In a closet stocked from end to end,
I sought a gem I could commend.
A slip of paper caught my eye,
Could it lead me to treasure nigh?

I raced through shoes and retro hats,
"More bling!" I cried, and tripped on mats.
I heard a laugh, it caused a stir,
My cousin's cat is such a blur!

With every flop and every slip,
The necklace tease is quite a trip.
Yet silver earrings jingle free,
Dancing off of a laughing tree!

Oh what fun in wild pursuit,
Of elegant dreams in sequined suit.
Though I may seek and run about,
It's laughter's glow that wins, no doubt!

Luminous Dreams in Motion

I set out on a sunny spree,
For something shiny just for me.
A glint above the garden gate,
Could this be luck? I truly wait!

The squirrels laughed, they held the score,
With acorns stacked and shouts galore.
I stumbled forth, a curious sight,
Chasing ribbons in golden light!

Around each twist and hidden nook,
With giggles loud, I take a look.
Though all I find are broken toys,
I can't help but share the joys!

In bright reflections, I will roam,
Creating fun, I feel at home.
With laughter ringing 'neath the stars,
I dance within a world of spar!

The Enchantment of a Jewel's Journey

In a box, it lies so bright,
A treasure that catches the light.
But oh, it rolls off the shelf,
To seek adventures by itself.

It bounced on a cat's tail, oh dear!
The feline gave chase with a cheer.
Around and around they spun wild,
While the neighbors looked on, beguiled.

Next stop, a puddle, what fun!
With a splash, it danced, oh what a run!
Reflecting giggles from all around,
A gem on the loose, joy unbound.

At last, it rolls to a child's hand,
With dreams of castles, so grand.
Who knew a jewel could bring such glee?
A whimsical tale, for you and me.

A Voyage to the Heart's Trinket

Glittering bright, lost in a sea,
Of socks and old toys, where can it be?
Diving deep through the fabric's maze,
It's on a quest for brighter days!

A sock puppet gangs up for a laugh,
Together they plan a silly path.
Through the laundry, they skip and twirl,
As the laughter of kids starts to whirl.

In the search for the heart's true bling,
They find a button that starts to sing.
"Oh, brave little pearl, don't lose your shine,
We'll find you a home, so just align!"

With friends, it finds its way back soon,
To a kid's palm, bright as the moon.
The journey's the magic, they'd all agree,
For treasures are fun when shared, oh me!

Moonlit Reflections of Dazzling Desires

Once, in the night, a sparkle took flight,
Wandering far, glowing so bright.
It danced with the stars in playful delight,
Playing hide and seek with the prowling night.

A raccoon spotted its shimmering glow,
Decided to join in the luminous show.
With a hop and a skip, he grabbed a nearby snack,
The jewel just rolled right off his back!

Down to a puddle where frogs do reside,
They croaked, "Oh look, what a sparkling guide!
Join in our leap and hop down the lane,
Let's splash in the moonlight, let's break every chain!"

As morning approached, their fun bid adieu,
With frog friends and a raccoon's crew.
The jewel found a home, though not at all grand,
In a joyful caper, it made its own band.

The Allure of Unseen Ornaments

A crown forgotten, lost in a box,
Now hidden beneath some old, dusty socks.
With a wiggle and jiggle, it starts to elope,
Planning a heist to grab all the hope!

Sneaking through doors, a bold masquerade,
Dressed up in laughter, a shimmering charade.
Rolling past clocks and fluffy old beds,
Where dreams and pastries are made for the heads.

"Oh look at me! I've sparkling charm!"
Said the crown as it waved with alarm.
"Join me, dear iron, we'll steal every show!
With laughter and joy, let's put on a glow!"

In the end, they pooled together to dance,
Jewelry from wonders, a whimsical trance.
For the earth shines brighter in a playful swirl,
With a crown full of dreams, let laughter unfurl!

The Fragments of Shining Whispers

In a world of sparkles and tease,
I stumbled on dreams with ease.
A gleam caught my eye, oh so bright,
I giggled and danced in delight.

The whispers of glimmering charms,
Wrapped around me, causing alarms.
A jump and a twirl, I took flight,
Chasing the shine into the night.

With my friends in a wild parade,
We searched for the glimmers, unafraid.
With every twist, the laughter grew,
And oh, the silliness that we knew.

But as the sparkles dimmed away,
We sat with our dreams in dismay.
With crumbs of jewels in our hands,
We laughed like fools on glittering sands.

Twinkling Threads of Destiny

A bag full of wishes, just so bright,
We skipped through the alleys of light.
With every twinkle, we lost our way,
But hilarity saved the day!

Caught in a web of shimmering fate,
Who knew links could grow so great?
We tumbled and tripped, a sight to see,
How fun it is to chase glee!

Each thread pulled us in merry spins,
And laughter echoed, where it begins.
The chase for glitter, a comic quest,
We found pure joy, that was the best.

As we twirled 'neath the splendid beams,
In the end, it was just silly dreams.
No treasure found, but memories gleamed,
A fun adventure, or so we deemed!

Germany's Treasure Trail of Dreams

With a map in hand and a wink,
We sauntered past the beer and drink.
Through castles and fields, we boldly strode,
Finding giggles on the winding road.

Bavarian hats and pretzels to munch,
We laughed so hard, it was a crunch.
As shiny baubles danced in our sight,
We couldn't stop, it felt so right.

Every corner turned was a new delight,
With treasures of laughter, oh what a sight!
In each hidden nook, joy would spark,
Our chase for smiles lit up the dark.

Yet the treasure was just a funny tale,
Of mishaps and giggles that would prevail.
In Germany's hug, we lost our fears,
With memories made, we drank our cheers!

The Ambivalence of a Glimmering Desire

In a world where the sparkles tease,
I pondered my wants with such ease.
A glint in the air, what could it be?
Was it treasure, or just pure glee?

With ambivalence wrapped in a fold,
I laughed at shiny things uncontrolled.
A dance with shadows, a flicker or two,
Each twinkle brought forth something new.

Friends by my side with jest and cheer,
We twisted with joy, released every fear.
As we leaped and twirled, the world became bright,
Chasing a whim just felt so right.

And when the bells chimed, our chase had no end,
For in laughter's embrace, we found a friend.
The desire was playful, a comical ride,
And in that moment, we felt so alive.

The Dance of Heirloom Strings

In a ballroom filled with gleam,
A necklace flutters like a dream,
It prances round on eager necks,
While we all slip on mismatched specs.

A twist and turn, it plays a game,
With every step, we shout its name,
Old Auntie Jo, she takes a leap,
The pearls go flying, oh how we peep!

The chandelier shakes with all the fun,
Our silly antics never done,
With every glance, a laugh we earn,
As beads of laughter wildly churn.

At midnight's chime, the lights will fade,
But in our hearts, the charm won't trade,
We dance until the night's last ring,
With treasures found in every fling.

Pursuit of the Midnight Gem

In shadows deep where mischief brews,
A sparkly trinket steals our views,
We dash and dart like crazy fools,
Through gardens filled with villain's tools.

A twist of fate, that shimmering thing,
Leads us on a wild, wacky fling,
With garden gnomes and prancing cats,
It's hard to focus on bling or chats.

We tumble down as laughter rolls,
Through flower beds, we lose our soles,
And bloomers worn are four sizes wide,
Yet there it shines, our pretty guide!

The sun comes up, our chase still true,
But dirt and grime were never due,
With giggles shared and tales of plight,
We find the gem, oh what a night!

Echoes of Elegance in Starlit Paths

Beneath the stars, a treasure glows,
A sparkling prize, as tension grows,
We tiptoe lightly, shivering glee,
As wind whispers hints of mystery.

With goofy grins, we stumble, sigh,
Forget our fears, just me and guy,
The moonlight's dance, a playful tease,
We chase it down with careless ease.

Our feet are sore, our hair's a mess,
But who would trade this silliness?
With gleeful yelps, we reach for stars,
And dodge the tree that bears our scars.

As dawn creeps near, we laugh and sing,
Two fools entwined where joy can cling,
The echoes fade, but in our heart,
The sparkle lasts, we'll never part.

Treasures Adrift on Serpent's Waves

A ship on waves we laugh and cheer,
With treasures glinting that draw near,
A necklace floats, a sly old tease,
While pirates groan with rattling knees.

The deck's a mess, with socks and hats,
Our search a muddle, full of spats,
We spot the gold! Oh, what a jest,
With me in charge, we're poorly blessed.

The sea turns wild with silly squawks,
While seagulls laugh in mocking flocks,
With tangled ropes and throwing nets,
It slips away, our biggest threat!

Yet on we sail through waves of fun,
With every blunder, more laughs spun,
For in this chase, what's prize or claim,
When fun's the treasure, and life's the game!

Adrift in Gleaming Echoes

In a world of glimmering dreams,
I dashed through sparkly seams.
Each step a curious affair,
What's that wobbling over there?

Charmed by glitter, I was lost,
Every shimmer, a hidden cost.
Tripped on laughter, fell on glee,
Lost my grip on reality!

My pockets filled with bright distraction,
But not a bit of my own satisfaction.
In this circus of shining grace,
I found only my goofball face!

A quest of whimsy, joy, and jest,
Who knew this mess would be the best?
Through life's maze, I'm just a sprite,
Adrift in echoes, day and night!

Pursuit of Celestial Charms

Dancing stars, a dizzy chase,
I ran in circles, what a race!
With every swirl, a laugh or two,
Catch a comet? Yes, I'll do!

Dodging moons and wobbly suns,
A tapestry of quirky runs.
Stumbling here and sliding there,
Who needs reason? I don't care!

Rainbows dangle just out of hand,
Like cotton candy, oh so grand!
Then I tripped on my own bright shoelace,
Tangled up in cosmic grace!

The universe winks with cheeky cheer,
While I flail, it's perfectly clear.
In pursuing charms that light my way,
I'm the punchline at the end of the day!

The Folly of Glittering Pursuits

A shining charm caught my eye,
Beneath the sun, I leapt to fly.
But in my haste, I tripped and rolled,
Finding myself in glittery gold!

Each gleam a laugh, each sparkle a tease,
Chasing folly like a floating breeze.
With laughter echoing in my ears,
I fell right down, consumed by cheers!

Oh, what a sight! A glittery mess,
Wrapped in jewels, a sparkly dress.
Yet beneath the bling, I found surprise,
The real fun shines in silly ties!

So here I am, in silly haste,
A jester lost in glamorous waste.
In folly's grip, may I remain,
Just a fool for laughter's gain!

A Tapestry of Longing

Stitches of dreams in every hue,
A fabric woven from the view.
Each thread a giggle, a bump, a sigh,
As I reach for wonders passing by!

In the tapestry of what I seek,
I stumbled on laughter, cheek to cheek.
A wish so bright, it made me trip,
With every tug, I lost my grip!

The longing thinned, like threads entwined,
When caught in laughter, light, and kind.
Glittering hopes danced out of reach,
Yet with each stumble, I learned to breach.

So here I dwell, within this weave,
Where silliness sprouts, and we believe.
In joy's embrace, I find my way,
A tapestry stitched with gleeful play!

Moonlit Trails of Forgotten Jewels

Under the glow of the silvery light,
Hilarity reigns, oh what a sight!
A clumsy raccoon with a shiny prize,
Dances around with glitter in its eyes.

Chasing shadows, they leap and bound,
Through the forest floor, cover ground.
A lost treasure from a prank gone wrong,
Laughter echoes, like a silly song.

A glimmer here, a sparkle there,
Squirrels giggle as they lay bare.
What was once grand turns to comedic gold,
In this night of antics, jubilantly bold.

So if you seek what once was fine,
Join the chaos, sip your wine.
For in the chase of whimsical fate,
Laughter's the jewel we all celebrate.

Reflections of a Forgotten Elegance

In the attic lies a dusty chest,
Full of memories, a jester's quest.
An old tiara, crooked and bent,
Dressed up a cat; now that's time well spent!

The mirror laughs with each silly glance,
As poor Mittens twirls in a dainty dance.
With every twist, the jewels do clank,
A royal feline, before we draw rank.

Forgotten elegance goes for a spin,
As laughter and jewels mix with a grin.
Gather your friends for one grand review,
Who thought diamonds could cause such a stew?

So let's toast to what's lost in the haze,
And the laughter from these strange, foolish days.
In reflections of elegance, chortles collide,
Where every heirloom tells tales of pride.

The Entrancing Glow of Longing

In the garden, a shimmer betrays,
A longing for bling that tickles the gaze.
Fireflies dancing, oh what a tease,
Chasing each spark with giggling ease.

A gnome with a hat, held up by a twig,
In a race for a trinket, oh! What a gig!
His cheeky grin, with mischief afoot,
Chasing the glow of a runaway foot.

Beneath the stars, the night turns absurd,
A necklace lies lost, but laughter's preferred.
Each stumble and tumble brings joy to the night,
Where jewels become jesters, twinkling with light.

So heed the call of folly and fun,
For treasures and giggles are never outdone.
In the entrancing glow, let your heart race,
In the hunt for bling, find your own happy place.

Enigma of the Shining Heirloom

An heirloom shining, a mystery wrapped,
But what's the fuss? Have we all been trapped?
In the kitchen, a shimmer caught the eye,
Was it a gem or the cat's food supply?

With magnifying glasses, we sleuth and we scowl,
Pondering over a forgotten growl.
Was it grand once, or just painted bright?
Turned into nonsense in the kitchen light!

A family heirloom? More like a joke,
Inside the pot? We all nearly choked.
Laughter erupts as we sift through the grime,
What's hidden within? Pure comedy in time!

So toast to the mystery, toast to the cheer,
For every big laugh holds a gem somewhere near.
In the enigma we're lost, yet so very found,
Where humor and heirlooms continue to abound.

Stolen Memories in Brilliant Hues

A sparkling gem, it took to flight,
Around my neck, oh what a sight!
But cats are sneaky, quick and spry,
They've whisked it off, oh me, oh my!

In party hats, they plot and scheme,
While I just stood, the fool, it seems.
With every pounce and playful paw,
My jewels parade—what a faux pas!

They wear my treasures like a crown,
I chase them up and down the town.
With twinkling eyes and tails a-fluff,
I leap and bound—this is quite tough!

Yet laughter rings where diamonds flew,
My stolen gems, a purr-fect crew.
In hues so bright, my heart does swell,
In all this chaos, I bid farewell!

The Prism of Fleeting Possessions

A silly dance on the kitchen floor,
I spotted something, oh! What's in store?
A glimmer caught beneath the chair,
I thought 'tis mine, in a moment rare!

But then a dog with mischief found,
Made off with my prize, oh what a sound!
He pranced about with jubilee,
While I was left to search with glee.

Through windows wide, he dashed away,
A prism of joy in his playful sway.
With every bark, the echoes flow,
A chase ensued; should I let it go?

But laughter chased the frights away,
His antics brightened up the day.
In fleeting moments, we are free,
Possessions lost, but joy is key!

Lattice of Light and Longing

In the garden, I spotted a glint,
A treasure bright, it made me squint.
But that sneaky squirrel, with twitchy tail,
Stole my jewels, what a grand trail!

Around the trees, I hopped and spun,
While he just laughed, oh what fun!
He juggled my gems, a sight to see,
In the daylight's dance, a fancy spree!

My friends all gathered, sporting grins,
As I played tag with fluff and fins.
With every leap, we'd snicker and giggle,
While the squirrel danced, doing a jiggle!

The lattice of light, a sight so bright,
In chase of a dream that took flight.
For laughter reigns where treasures bounce,
In moments shared, we all pronounce!

Sirens Beneath the Surface

Oh, the allure that comes with shine,
Like sirens calling from the brine.
I dove into the depths with glee,
But fishes laughed; they'd captured me!

With bubbles swirling, they twisted around,
While I reached out for shiny found.
But slippery scales and wriggly fins,
Dodged every greet and clink of spins!

I surfaced, gasping with wild surprise,
A school of fish, oh how they rise!
They flaunted jewels like they were stars,
As I waved goodbye from afar.

Yet in this ocean of playful jest,
I swam with laughter, feeling blessed.
For memories made from under the wave,
Are much more fun than things we crave!

A Dance in the Moonlight

Beneath the glow of silver beams,
A troupe of clowns with silly dreams.
They twirl and spin, a goofy sight,
Chasing trinkets all through the night.

With every step, they trip and fall,
Giggles break out; they can't stand tall.
Yet treasures glimmer in their eyes,
As they leap and bound to the skies.

A sparkly thing rolls down the hill,
They tumble after, laughter to spill.
A wild red nose lost in the chase,
Their dance unfolds in a joyous space.

In the end, they find charms galore,
But oh, the fun was worth much more!
With a wink and nod, the night they take,
For friendship shines more than a fake.

Echoes of Shimmering Desires

In a quirky shop of wobbly wares,
A crowd of jesters with wild stares.
They squeal and shout at shiny things,
Like children dreaming of fairy wings.

One slips on marbles, it's quite the sight,
They roll and giggle, a comic flight.
A dazzling trinket sits on a shelf,
But wait! Joe's stuck, can't free himself!

Chasing after banter, they trip and shout,
As bead necklaces sway in and out.
Their laughter echoes, fills up the room,
As jokes and gems create the bloom.

"What if it's cursed?" one nervously quips,
They whisper rumors with wiggly hips.
With shiny delights, they play hide and seek,
Yet it's their fun that makes them unique!

Treasure Beyond the Horizon

On a hillside crawling with glittery charm,
A motley crew with a cheeky arm.
They stumble over buckets of gold,
But they're really just laughing, or so I'm told.

"Look there!" yells Tim, with a grand old plea,
It's just a tin can; they all disagree.
They roll and tumble down the slope,
With goofy grins, they chase their hope.

The sun sets low with a comedic fling,
As tumbling treasures make them sing.
"Oh, what's that shiny?" one cries with glee,
It's just a hot dog wrapper, oh dear me!

But in each moment, joy they plug,
For laughter's the true treasure that's snug.
Digging through happiness up to the top,
Their antics continue, they'll never stop!

The Allure of Hidden Gems

In a garden filled with quirky stones,
A band of friends – all silly clones.
They dig with glee, each shout rings clear,
"Did I find one? Nope, it's my old beer!"

Through bushes and vines, they search with flair,
One's in a costume; what a funny pair!
All glitter and giggles; they sparkle and tease,
Like kids at play, they're just trying to please.

A glimmer appears, hearts beat with hope,
But alas! It's merely soap on a rope.
Yet laughter erupts, filling the air,
As they fall in puddles, without a care.

They find gems of joy, those moments pure,
In the treasure of laughter, they find the cure.
With smiles galore, they dance to their tune,
For happiness sparkles like light of the moon.

Glinting Memories in the Dark

Underneath the moonlit sky,
A sparkle caught my wandering eye.
I leapt and tripped, oh what a sight!
The raccoons laughed, 'What a night!'

Running fast, I lost my shoe,
In a puddle, a strange goo!
What was that? A necklace shine?
Or just a frog? Oh, never mind!

I swung around, a dizzy spin,
In search of treasures deep within.
The ground was soft, my giggles loud,
While planets twirled beneath the cloud.

So here we dance, the stars above,
Playing games, and all for fun.
The memories twinkle, bright and stark,
As I prance beneath the dark.

Unraveling Threads of Desire

A quest began with every twist,
In a shop where fate's a list.
I pulled at strings with silly zeal,
'Twas grand, but oh, the wheels did squeal!

A colorful mess upon the floor,
A necklace dreamer, wanting more.
With every tug, the laughter grew,
Oh, the shopkeeper just fumed, who knew?

I strung together socks and keys,
With beads that spark like summer bees.
What's a necklace, but endless glee?
Now it's a fashion spree for me!

So here's to threads that weave and heart,
Together, we'll never part.
In tangled joy, we find our way,
In this playful thread ballet.

Jewel of the Heart's Compass

A goofy grin, I search around,
In every nook, no gem is found.
Map in hand, I take a leap,
Storm clouds chase me, but I don't weep.

Navigating through the mud,
With squirrels giggling, isn't it good?
A sparkly gem glints from a tree,
But it's just a nut, oh woe is me!

Through bushes thick, I leap and bound,
With vision sharp, I'm glory-bound.
The squirrels nod, "Keep going, mate!"
The jewel lies behind the gate!

I find the prize—a chocolate piece,
With laughter ringing, who would cease?
In silly quests, we find our way,
A heart's compass leads to play.

The Allure of Untamed Brilliance

In the park, I spy a flash,
I trip and fall, with quite a crash!
A necklace, no! A shiny toy,
My laughter rings, oh, what a joy!

Bouncing balls and runaway kites,
Swirling chaos, such fun delights.
But what's this glare? I double back,
A dog with bling leads our pack!

Chasing shadows, giggles join,
We race around a garden coin.
A touch of nature, bling in sight,
I dabble with rocks, all feels just right!

So here we are, lost in this game,
With friends and laughter, never the same.
In untamed brilliance, we will stay,
For shiny things lead us to play.

The Call of the Dazzling Horizon

In a thrift shop I spied, a bright trinket bright,
A glimmering promise, oh what a sight.
Yet as I reached out, my shoe gave a squeak,
I knocked over a vase, what a wacky week!

With laughter and gasps, the crowd all turned,
'Is that a rare gem?' said one, quite concerned.
A dog chased my heels, I stumbled and spun,
Glimmers of laughter, oh what fun had begun!

Out in the sun, I danced with delight,
The trinket still twinkled, such a silly sight.
With friends all around, we giggled and played,
And forgot about treasures, the price never paid.

But there in the chaos, a glint caught my eye,
A shiny old spoon that just seemed to fly.
We laughed at our dreams, so whimsical, so bright,
For gems made of laughter are the true delight!

Secrets Beneath the Velvet Sky

Under the stars, where secret dreams bloom,
I found a lost pendant, amidst the night's gloom.
But then a raccoon, with too much ambition,
Decided to claim it, what a funny mission!

Running and tumbling, my heart pumped with zest,
I bargained with rodents, oh what a jest!
With my flashlight flickering, I crouched low and sly,
Trying to negotiate with a twinkle in my eye.

The moon watched in giggles as I told my odd tale,
Of critters and treasures and a glimmering trail.
In the end, I found joy in the chase and the light,
More laughter than jewels made this evening so bright.

So here's to the secrets that nighttime reveals,
In the grand tapestry of what life conceals.
For diamonds are fun but they come with their tricks,
And laughter's the gem that forever just sticks!

Lost in a Sea of Sparkling Wishes

On a beach made of wishes, I lost my last thought,
A necklace of bubbles, look at what I sought!
But the tide pulled it under, just as I waved,
Now I'm left here, feeling quite enslaved!

With a shovel in hand, I dug deep in the sand,
Where fish laughed in bubbles, not quite what I planned.
I imagined the treasures, the glimmers and glows,
But all I unearthed were old flip-flops and toes.

Seagulls squawked loudly, a cacophony bright,
As I waded through waves, what a comical sight!
The ocean just giggled, it's all just a game,
Who knew chasing wishes was so full of fame?

In a net filled with laughter, I finally found peace,
Buried in nonsense, my troubles released.
For sparkling wishes go far beyond bling,
It's the joy of the journey that makes my heart sing!

Shadows of Shimmering Secrets

In the attic of dreams, I shuffled about,
Finding some glitter, filled with a clout.
A box full of shadows, all shimmery bright,
I tripped on a dragon, what a comical sight!

As dust bunnies laughed from their cozy retreats,
I battled the treasures, exchanging my feats.
With a wink and a nod, I fended them off,
'This shiny old brooch isn't yours to scoff!'

The secrets around me did giggle and twirl,
As I slipped on a bracelet, I began to swirl.
A dance in the dark, with socks on my feet,
I pranced like a peacock, oh what a neat feat!

So here's to the shadows, so silly and sly,
In the world of treasure, where laughter can fly.
For when those secrets shimmer, and give me a wink,
I find that joy happens, quicker than you think!

A Glimpse of Timeless Beauty

In a shop filled with bling, oh so bright,
I spotted a gem that lit up the night.
It shimmered and winked, a sly little tease,
I laughed at its charm, oh, do as you please!

With a twist and a turn, it danced on the shelf,
A diva of jewels, proud of itself.
I reached for the treasure, but it slipped away,
And laughed as it giggled, "Not today!"

The sales lady chuckled, quite in on the game,
As I stumbled and fumbled, feeling quite lame.
With every misstep, I knew I was bound,
To track down that bauble, all over this town!

Yet every detour would brighten my chase,
Through laughter and banter, I lost all my grace.
A treasure that's worthy, though it's just a tease,
Is better when chased with a giggle and ease!

Reflection on a Swirling Tide

Down by the shore, waves roll with a cheer,
I spotted a sparkle, was it drawing near?
I jumped like a fish, with a splash and a dive,
But alas, it was just a bottle, alive!

It tumbled and swirled in the foamy green sea,
I chased it around, oh, the joy that it be!
But as I leaned closer, I thought it was wise,
To ponder the bait—and to cover my eyes!

For deep in the waters, a treasure entranced,
Might just be a shell that mischievously pranced.
The laughter of gulls echoed clear as the day,
As I rolled and I tumbled, still hoping to play!

In the quest for the shiny, I learned with delight,
That the journey's the fun, not just the blinged sight.
With each wave that crashed, and each cackle that flew,
I danced with the tide, and got soaked, how 'bout you?

The Dance of Distant Diamonds

In a ballroom of laughter, the gems take the floor,
They twirl and they spin, like never before.
With sparkles and glimmers, they join in the fun,
Each one a little diva, second to none!

A ruby winks bright, a sapphire does sway,
While emeralds gossip, come join in the fray.
I attempted a slide, but tripped on my shoe,
And laughed as my dance turned a bit askew!

With each glint and shine, I'm lost in the show,
These stones got more moves than I surely know.
Yet among all this chaos, I finally see,
The true joy—a giggle shared with blinged glee!

So let the diamonds dance and let the laughter flow,
In the ball of delight, it's a dazzling show.
I might not be graceful, nor fancy and sleek,
But there's fun in the chase, and that's what I seek!

In Pursuit of Eternal Sparkle

I woke up one morning, feeling quite bold,
To seek out the bright, the shiny, the gold.
I donned my best shoes, and my hat with a flair,
Not knowing adventure would soon break my care!

From markets to gardens, I scurried and sped,
With dreams of the shimmer dancing in my head.
But amid all the chaos, I found quite a sight,
A cat on a wall with a necklace so bright!

It purred and it pranced like the queen of the street,
I begged it to share its shiny gold treat.
But with a flick of its tail, it jumped up and ran,
Leaving me in a giggle, an unfortunate plan!

With laughter as currency, I'll never be sad,
For every wild chase makes my life quite a lad.
So, here's to the treasure that never stays still,
In the quest for the sparkle, I'm high on the thrill!

Fantasies Wrapped in Golden Chains

In a shop adorned with glittery dreams,
I tripped on my hopes, or so it seems.
With a twinkle here and a clasp so grand,
I waved goodbye to my empty hand.

Each sparkly bauble made me giggle,
As I fumbled and flailed, it was quite the wiggle.
But once on display, oh what a sight!
I wore my mishaps like jewels in the night.

A friend at my side, laughed till we cried,
My necklace a serpent, it slipped, it sighed.
With laughter and joy, we tangled in fun,
That golden chain turned into a run.

In the end, I found a charm so divine,
Silly and awkward, but oh, it was fine.
Wrapped in laughter, like a good friend should,
These fantasies shined, and oh how they would!

The Treasure Map of a Heart's Desire

With a map made of dreams and a wink of fate,
I set out on a quest that felt just great.
Each 'X' marked a spot where giggles appeared,
My heart leading me on, and I was not feared.

Through jungles of laughter and valleys of glee,
I searched for the prize, though it hid from me.
Every twist and turn brought a fanciful tale,
Of sparrows and goldfish, and a pig in a sail.

At the end of the path, what treasures lay there?
A sparkling bauble? Nah, just a teddy bear!
Yet in all the chaos, my heart danced with cheer,
For the map led me here, and that's all I hold dear.

So I hoisted the bear, my true treasured sight,
With a smile on my face, everything felt right.
A journey so silly, with joy it conspired,
Sharing laughter and dreams, my heart's true desire.

Whispers of Precious Threads

In a world spun of whimsy, I found my own thread,
Each color and shimmer, a tale to be said.
With whispers of gold and a twinkle of pearls,
I danced round the aisles, like a top in a whirl.

A friend nudged me gently, her giggle was bright,
As I tried on a necklace that sparkled with light.
Yet it tangled my hair in a fashionable mess,
I chuckled aloud, 'Well, I must confess!'

We laughed at the chain's little playful tricks,
As it looped around fingers, like mischievous licks.
With each playful twist, came a giggle and sigh,
'Who knew fashion could be such a sly guy?'

With layers of laughter, we wrapped up the day,
In threads of sweet joy, we danced all the way.
So here's to the trinkets and giggles galore,
In the whispers of threads, there's always much more!

The Glimmering Pursuit

On a quest for a shimmer, I strutted with pride,
With visions of jewels swirling deep inside.
But the bouncy little dog saw my glimmering bait,
And off it raced, like it couldn't wait.

Oh, the chase turned into a whimsical spree,
I stumbled, I laughed, oh how silly to be!
The leash tangled 'round my leg with a twist,
I grabbed at my dreams but they played at a tryst.

A crowd gathered round, giggling at me,
As my pursuit turned into a circus—quite free!
With the dog as my guide, we danced near the stalls,
Amidst the loud laughter and "Look at those falls!"

At the end of the day, just dog treats I'd find,
Yet, the joy of the chase left me blissfully blind.
For in every mishap, a tale takes its flight,
In glimmering pursuits, oh, what pure delight!

www.ingramcontent.com/pod-product-compliance
Lightning Source LLC
Chambersburg PA
CBHW062110280426
43661CB00086B/441